I0487371

Cashing in on Google

How to Use Google to get more traffic, and more sales, without spending a dime

by Jinger Jarrett

If you need support, please contact Jinger Jarrett at:
http://www.jingerjarrett.com/support/

Published by Create Space
ISBN: 1440415021
EAN-13: 9781440415029

Table of Contents

Part 1
High Traffic Marketing Site

A lot has been said lately about using videos to promote your products, and you can find plenty of ebooks to buy about promoting your videos on Google.

However, there is far more to Google than just video. Google has tons of different ways you can promote your business and make money from it.

What I want to do is show you all of the different ways you can use Google to promote your business. Follow each of these steps. Work one section of Google at a time.

Some of these things may not apply. If you promote only affiliate links, you'll have a hard time promoting with Google unless you use Google Groups.

If you have your own website, then you'll find plenty of ways to promote your business.

Again, work the steps. If you can only do one section at a time, then do that, but work your way through all of this until you have used every Google service possible to promote your business.

Now let's get started.

Marketing With Google

The first place you will want to start is on the Google services page. This is so you can see all of the services Google has to offer.

Your first step will be to decide which of these services you want to use.

Google Services –

http://www.google.com/services/

You can see all of Google's services here:
http://www.google.com/intl/en/options/#utm_mediu m=et&utm_source=bizsols&utm_campaign=more

To make it easy on you, we will start with the first, and easiest service, Google Sitemaps.

Google Sitemaps –

http://www.google.com/webmasters/tools/login

There is really nothing difficult about getting your site submitted to Google. The internet marketing "gurus" often talk about getting in the "backdoor" of Google. However, this may include blackhat marketing techniques that can get you banned. The best way to use Google is to follow Google's instructions, go in the front door, and you'll get in Google quickly and easily. Once you're in, then you can work on optimizing your website so you can raise your rankings.

Now, although you can use the regular submission, the problem is that Google will get around to spidering your site when it is ready.

Google contains billions of pages, and even with all of the resources Google has, it still takes a little time to spider and respider all of those pages.

So, if you want to get your site spidered rather quickly, and you want a set and forget approach, then Google Sitemaps is the way to do it.

Your first step is to actually create your sitemap. The best tool I have found for doing this is **Sitemapspal** – http:// www.sitemapspal.com/. This tool will allow you to create a sitemap you can use with both Yahoo and Google.

All you have to do is enter the URL of the site you want to spider. Once it has spidered your site, then you copy and paste the code it generates into a text document. Save the file as sitemap.xml.

Next, upload the sitemap using your FTP client. You can also log into your control panel at the backend of your website and upload it. Make sure you upload it into the root directory of your site. The root directory for your site is the directory your domain points to.

For example, my domain jingerjarrett.com is in the root directory for my web hosting. This means the folder is public_html. The folder for my smallbusinesshowto.com website is smallbusinesshowto.com, and so if I were creating a sitemap for this site, I would upload the sitemap into the smallbusinesshowto.com folder.

Once you have uploaded your sitemap to your site directory, your next step is to add it to Google. To do this, you will need a text editor to make a blank html document to upload to your website. (Google and Yahoo both will show you what code you need to add to your site and how you can verify your website. You can use either the file verification method, which they will tell you what to name the file, or the code method which you add to the header of your page.)

To upload your sitemap to Google, you will need a Gmail account. If you don't have one, then you can sign up for one for free. **Gmail – http://gmail.google.com/**

Once you have your Gmail account, and you have verified it, then go to the Google Sitemaps page and log in with your new account.

At the top of the screen, you will see a bar that says, "Add site". Type in the URL of your site there exactly the way Google shows you how to do it and hit "OK".

If none of your pages are included in the Google index, you will need to verify your site.

Click verify your site.

It will give you two choices on how to verify your site. You can either add a tag to the header of your main page, or you can create a blank html file. The system will tell you what to name this file. You will need to upload this file to your website. Create your blank document by opening a text document. Copy and paste the name of the document, and then save as. Save the blank document into the folder for your website on your computer. Then you need to upload this to your site.

Once you have verified, then you will need to add your sitemap. Click on the tab that says "Sitemaps". Then you will type the path to your sitemap. For my website smallbusinesshowto.com, the path is **http://www.smallbusinesshowto.com/sitemap.xml**. (If you want to see what a sitemap looks like, you can click on mine). :)

Follow the prompts. This is very step by step, and it will tell you what you need to do. Once you've completed the steps, it will show the status of your sitemaps.

How long will it take for your site to show up in Google? Depending on how big it is, about 24 hours. This is what the internet marketing "gurus" charge you $97 or more to tell you.

Google Base - http://base.google.com/base

Google Base is a somewhat more advanced way of getting your website indexed because it allows you to organize your content into different categories, i.e., articles, products, etc. In order to use Google Base, you will need to create a feed for what you are trying to index. This is really much easier than it sounds. This task is a little more time consuming, but it's worth it to help raise your rankings in the search engines, make sure all of your pages are indexed, and get more traffic.

If you have 10 or fewer items you want to add, then all you have to do is log into Google Base, fill out a web form for each item you would like to post, and then post the item. If you have more than 10 items, it's better if you create a feed.

Your first step will be to create a feed what you plan to index. If you plan to index your articles for example, you will need a tool that allows you to index your articles.

The best tool for helping you create your feeds is Feed Publish - http://www.feedpublish.com/. You can sign up for a free account and create as many feeds as you wish. If you want to use software to do this, then I recommend the free tool **RSS Writer** – http://www.phelios.net/rss-writer.html. This tool is available in both PC and MAC, and it allows you to create an RSS feed for your site if you don't have one. You can also use it to create the feeds you need to organize your content. Once you've created your feed, if you use RSS Writer, you'll need to upload this to your site. Give it a descriptive name because you can't call it sitemap.xml. For example, if you are creating a feed of articles, name it articles.xml. If you are using Feed Publish, then you'll need to use the link they give you.

Depending on how much content you have, it make a take a little while to create your feeds. However, if you really want to organize your content, this is the way to do it.

Once you have created your feed, or if you have less than 10 items, sign into Google Base.

Once you have logged in, you will be given a choice: choose your own feed type, or create one.

On the next page, you will need to add some information before you can publish your feed.

Select a title for the feed. Make sure that the title includes your keywords. In other words, write a keyword rich title. Since you should be the author of this feed, add your name or your company name.

You can remove the source unless you are a big name site.

Next, write a description of what your feed is about. This should include your most important keywords. Write a good description here.

At the bottom, you will need to add the link to your feed. If you have downloaded it onto your computer, you can attach it this way. If it is a feed from the Web, type the path of the feed.

For example:

http://www.yourdomainname.com/feed.xml

The feed format should be in XML. This is a very search engine friendly form of code.

Before submitting, I would recommend you preview your information. Once you've previewed your information, and everything is correct, then you can publish your feed. You're done!

The good thing about Google Base is that you can add your content even if you don't have a website. Also, by adding your content to Google Base, especially your products, you will be included in **Google Product Search**, which is the Google Marketplace. http://www.google.com/products. If you'd like to add your products to Google Product Search, you can add it here:

http://www.google.com/base/help/sellongoogle.html. The format is very similar to creating a Google Base account.

Google Blog Search -

http://www.google.com/help/about_blogsearch.html

Google Blog Search is the section of Google that lists nothing but blogs. What makes this service so great, other than that you can get your blog listed there, is that if you need to search for blogs on specific topics, this is a great place to search.

The reason is that Google allows you to use the same search techniques on Blog Search that you use on their regular search.

Why is this important?

Have you ever searched a site like Technorati, or other Blog Search site? It's very time consuming to find what you are looking for simply because most of these sites don't have a search that works the same way as Google.

Let me give you an example:

Say you are looking for information on internet marketing or some other broad topic. The problem is that when you search these sites, you'll get all kinds of results based on the tags, or keywords that the blogger has chosen for a particular post. If the blogger doesn't know how to properly tag, or if the posts aren't tagged, then you'll have to dig through a lot of unrelated results to find what you're looking for.

Not so with Google. With Google, you simply type in the keywords you're looking for. If you want tighter results, you put quotes around your keywords.

Now, to get into Blog Search, you need to be included in Google. As I showed you before, you can do this by using a sitemap. You can also do this by adding your blog to your Google News Page.

The easiest way to do this is if you have the My Google button on your website where you can subscribe by RSS.

If you don't have these buttons on your website, the easiest way to add them is to use a service like **Feedburner**, http://www.feedburner.com/ . You copy your feed and add it to this site (You will need an account, but it's free). Once you've added your feed, then you can create your buttons. All you have to do is copy and paste the code onto your blog page, and you're done.

This will help you in getting into Blog Search, but if you want Blog Search updated as you update your blog, then you need to go one step further.

If you have a Blogger blog, then you don't really need to do anything because Google owns Blogger. If you don't, then I suggest you set up an automatic ping to let Google know that you've updated your blog. This is in addition to submitting your sitemap.

I use Wordpress, and so it only takes a couple of minutes to set this up.

First, you need to go to Google and get the API for Google so that you can set up your blog to automatically ping Google. You can use the link below to do this:

Setting Up Automatic Ping -

http://www.google.com/help/blogsearch/pinging_API.html

Where is says RPC endpoint, you want to copy this URL. This is the URL to the API. The URL is:

http://blogsearch.google.com/ping/RPC2.

Log into the backend of your Wordpress blog and click on Settings. (You can do this with any blog client that allows you to add your ping services. Check with the service you use to find out how to do this.)

Now, if you don't have this plugin installed, you will need to install it first. The plugin you need is called: **Max BlogPress Ping Optimizer:**

http://www.maxblogpress.com/plugins/mpo/. You can get this plugin for free. (You will need to subscribe to their ezine in order to activate it, but it's free.)

If you haven't already installed the plugin, upload it to your Wordpress installation, and then go to the Plugins tab on your blog. Enable the plugin.

Next, you will need to go to the Settings tab on your blog. Click on the tab that says MBP Ping Optimizer. You will need to copy and paste the URL I gave you above into the list of ping services and then click Save Settings. This will notify Google every time you post to your blog.

Once you have uploaded the plugin, activated it, and set up a ping to Google, you're ready to go. Your blog will take care of the rest.

What will this do for your blog?

First, there's a problem with the way that Wordpress pings. If you write a lot of posts, or you have to update your posts, then you'll have a lot of problems, and you can even get banned because Wordpress is set to ping every time you make an update or post. This causes your Wordpress blog to overping, and it looks like you are spamming.

The plugin will change the way your Wordpress blog pings, and it will ping according to what type of post it is, not every time you do an update. This plugin corrects the automatic ping that Wordpress does with every update.

Once you've set up your ping service, you're done.

If you don't want to bother with these, there is a service you can use to manually ping your blog so that the blog services know that your site has been updated. If you use this service, then make sure you don't ping your blog more than once every 30 minutes. Otherwise, this can get you banned from using this service to ping your blog.

Ping-o-Matic! – http://www.pingomatic.com/

Ping your blog regularly, at least every time you post. Not only does this help the blog services keep your listings updated, but it helps with the search engines too.

Google Book Search - http://books.google.com/intl/en/googlebooks/publishers.html

Unless you are selling a book, you can skip this section as this applies to book authors. Currently Google has a Book Search section that you can use to sell more of your books.

When this service first debuted, a lot of critics said that Google would make it harder for authors to sell books, and book authors would be making a mistake adding their books.

However, if you read the terms on this section, Google is very clear about what content they post, and publishers and book authors have complete control here.

Now, if you sell your books on Lulu the way I do, then all you have to do is add Google Book Search to your shopping cart after you buy Global Distribution. You will need to log into your account at Lulu. Click the My Account tab. You will see a list of your most recent titles. Next to the title that you want to add to Google Book Search will be a link for you to add Google Book

Search to your shopping cart. This service is free when you buy Global Distribution, but you have to add it to your shopping cart in order to get this. This is because your book belongs to you, and authors ultimately have control over whether or not to add their books.

If you plan to submit your book yourself, you will need to go to Google Book Search. You will need an ISBN to do this (this comes with your Global Distribution if you are using Lulu). Otherwise you will need to purchase an ISBN unless your publisher has one. If you have a publisher, then it's a good idea to check with them to see if they have already submitted your title to Google.

Click on the link that says Information for Publishers. You will need a Gmail account for this. You will also need to apply for an account for this service.

Once you've applied for your account, and you've been accepted into the program, then you can start adding your books. (This takes time. All accounts are manually approved, so you will have to hear from Google before you can start adding your books).

You will need an ISBN for each of your books. Google doesn't accept ebooks or other digital products.

Google Checkout - https://checkout.google.com/

Google Checkout is designed for those who don't have a merchant account and want to sell online. In truth, it's actually a competitor of Pay Pal. The advantage of using Google Checkout is that it makes your products available to everyone, and it also gets you included in Google. You can sell just about any type of product you want, both digital and physical. Make sure you check the terms of service at Google so you are only selling products and services they allow.

Now, the drawback to Google Checkout is that you need a shopping cart to automate the process. Google recommends several services. However, if you have a shopping cart on your site already, I would suggest you integrate Google Checkout with it so that you don't end up racking up a lot of fees.

Like some of the services with Google, you have to request an account here. Having a Gmail account isn't enough, although you can use Gmail to log in.

Your first step is to go to the main page of Checkout and scroll down to where you see information for sellers. Click on this link. It will take you to a new log in page. You can log in here and then sign up for your account. You will get instant approval.

Now, if you are selling digital goods, I would recommend that you create an HTML order form for your site. You will need to process your orders manually, but you will have to do that anyway.

If you are selling digital goods, and you want to automate your transactions, then I would recommend you use a service like **Pay Loadz** – http://www.payloadz.com/.

The reason is that this service allows you to offer both Pay Pal and Google Checkout, and you can automate the entire process so that you don't have to worry about digital delivery. It also allows you to offer an affiliate program, and you will be included in their store, as well as Ebay Stores and auctions. You don't need a website to do this.

The drawback here however, is that you can only sell digital goods, not physical goods. (If you want to offer an affiliate program and sell digital and physical goods, I would recommend **Pay Dot Com**: http://www.paydotcom.com).

You have two ways to upgrade with Pay Loadz: percentage of sales, or a monthly fee. If you don't have any money starting out, definitely do the percentage of sales because this way you can pay as you go. To me, this seems the way to go anyway.

Pay Loadz also offers an extensive help file to help you in integrating both Pay Pal and Google Checkout into your site, so you can actually use this site to integrate both programs and sell using both methods.

Now, if you decide to use the Pay Loadz option, you'll need to set up an account. You will add your product and download information here. Once you've set this up, then you will need to log into your Google Checkout account and follow the instructions for integrating with Pay Loadz. (Instructions on how to do this are included in the Pay Loadz help).

This way, you can sell digital goods and have automatic delivery. If you don't do this, and you get a lot of orders, then you could end up spending a lot of time processing orders. I don't know about you, but I'd rather be doing something else, and if you can't offer the digital download immediately, it will definitely cut your sales.

Finally, Google does offer several recommended shopping cart systems you can use to integrate into your sites. You'll find more information on which systems Google suggests in the help section: **https://checkout.google.com/support/sell/**.

Google Directory - http://www.google.com/dirhp

Google also offers a directory. They are affiliated with the Open Directory Project.

The purpose here is to organize all of the information on the Web. You will want to submit your site to this directory in addition to getting your site listed in Google. Submitting to the ODP will give you a high ranking one way backlink.

Your first step is to find the right category to submit to. You will want to carefully browse this site. If you choose the wrong category, or the editors feels your site is wrong for the category, they will reject your site, and you won't ever know. Since this is a volunteer project, it takes time to get accepted, and the last thing you want to do is alienate the editors

So, what you will need to do is drill down until you find the correct category for your site. Once you've found the right category, click on the Submit Site at the bottom of the page.

When submitting your site, it's important to write a good, keyword rich, description of your site. However, you want to make it sound natural. Also, don't write a description that sounds like an ad or sales letter. The editor will reject it outright, and you'll have to start all over.

Once you've submitted your site(s), then move on. It will take awhile to get accepted. Check back in about eight weeks. Do a search for your site. If you still haven't been accepted, keep trying.

Google Local -
http://www.google.com/local/add/businessCenter?
gl=US&hl=en-US

Google Local allows you to create a listing for your business. This is especially important if you offer services, as well as a physical presence in the real world.

Getting started with this is easy.

Click the link above, and it will take you to the main page. If you haven't signed in, you will need to sign in.

Once you've signed in, click the link that says Add/Edit Your Business. You will be taken to the next page where you can add your business information.

What's important here is to make sure you add complete and accurate information about your business. Don't write an ad. Include all of the information that's required so you have a clear and succinct listing.

You will also need to validate your listing in order for it to appear. You can do this either by phone or postcard. Once you've validated your listing, you will appear in the Local Search.

Google News - http://news.google.com/

There are several things that you can do with Google News that will really help you with your business.

First, you can add your RSS feeds for your blogs, as well as your sites. (If you don't have a feed, use the Site Map maker listed earlier to create your feeds, and then personalize your page at Google.)

Second, you can use Google News to tell you what's hot in your industry. Google News is an extremely comprehensive news resource, and to me, it's the best one to use to do your research. It includes over 4,500 news resources, including newspapers, blogs, article directories, and other resource sites.

So, if you want to promote your business, and you want to find places to submit your press releases, articles, and other promotional materials, start here

(Although PR Web can help you get listed here, you will want to use this site to help you find other resources. One of the most overlooked promotional resources is hometown newspapers. Create a local hook, and it can create a lot of business for you).

The way to use this is to start by doing a search. If you have articles you want to get listed in Google News, then you will need to do a search using your search term and the word articles.

For example, I am searching for directories that accept internet marketing articles, so I do a search for internet marketing articles.

Here are some of the results:

News Wire (press releases) – This is a paid service, and they accept press releases. You are looking for free resources to get your articles indexed, so skip this one.

People's Daily Online – Chinese newspaper. Might be good if you live in China, or you want to submit news related to China.

Small Business Informer – Accepts press releases. I believe they also accept business articles.

Promotion World – Accepts articles on internet marketing and promotion. Their latest article to come up is mine. :)

Much of what you will find is news stories and press releases. That's why it's so important to include press releases as part of your marketing efforts. However, there are sites that are included here that offer articles, and it's a quick and easy way for you to get included.

A tip here: if you like to write reviews, then join Blog Critics. You can contact them to become a writer for them. You can write as many, or as few, reviews as you like. Not only is this an easy way to get included in Google News, but they offer front page feature for really good reviews, as well as a chance at syndication.

Here is an example of a review that I wrote on the book, "Flags of Our Fathers". It was picked up for syndication: **http://blogcritics.org/archives/2006/10/14/145425.php**. This review was also a main page feature.

If you hate writing, then these techniques probably won't work for you. I would suggest something like Google Adwords, if you don't mind paying for advertising, or something like that.

You'll find the tools you need to conduct effective Google Adwords campaigns in the resources section. These are all free, and I scoured the internet to find them for you. Also, these are really the only tools you need to use to use Google Adwords. (Please note, if you decide to use Google Adwords, Pay Loadz offers a $50 credit for this program. This will give you a chance to try it out first so you don't waste your money getting good ads).

Finally, one of the best ways to learn how to write good Google Ads is to simply study Google Ads and see which ads are coming up for your search. Google ranks ads according to how well they are converting, not how much the advertiser paid to have them placed there.

Google Video - http://video.google.com/

You Tube – http://www.youtube.com/

There are a couple of different ways that you can use these sites.

First, you can post the videos to your blog. You don't have to download anything. All you have to do is create an account, log in, and then copy and paste some code into your website page to display the video. I did this with my blog.

Although it's a little hard to find videos to post, occasionally a good one comes up. You can see an example of this here: http://www.askjinger.com/writing/free-video-on-self-publishing/

The second way to use video is to create your own. You can use a simple tool like **Cam Studio**, http://www.camstudio.org/. This is a free video creation tool. It also offers a comprehensive FAQ on how you can use it to make good videos here: http://www.camstudio.org/faq.htm. This tutorial will solve an problems you may have in creating your videos.

Once you've created a video, you'll need to log into your You Tube account and upload your video. You will need to go to the link at the top that says My Account.

Use this page to upload your videos, as well as create your channel. Your channel is your page on You Tube. This is where you want to add your details about your business, as well as your link to your website. This is very important because it can allow you to promote your business.

Add the appropriate information to your channel, and update all of the settings in the Channel. You will find the link to this at the bottom of your account page.

You can see the channel I have created here: http://youtube.com/jejarrett.

You should also add your video to Google Video.

Google Groups - http://groups.google.com/

Marketing on groups is very similar to marketing on forums. You find discussion groups on your topic, join, and post your messages.

The advantage of using groups over forums is that you can quickly post your messages through email. By receiving messages in email, you can read your messages online or offline in your email client. It's easier to scan email messages to choose the ones you want to read, and depending on what types of groups you're subscribed to, you can use software to post to your groups.

Your first step to getting started with groups is to find groups you are interested in. Like posting to forums, you need to do a search for the right groups. You will also need to decide which groups you want to join based on the criteria you are searching for.

Like forums, you want groups that are active. It's not enough to post your messages so that you can get listed in the search engines. You want actual readers. You also want to join groups that have a lot of members. It's also no good if no one is reading your messages.

The advantage of using Google Groups is that you can do the same type of tight searches that you use in their search engines. This means you can put quotes around your search terms to get more relevant results. With Google Groups, you can also browse groups by the number of members they have. This way, you can quickly find the most active groups.

Another advantage to Google Groups is that you can get help on specific tools you are using within Google. Many of the answers here will come from Google employees, so you don't have to worry about them trying to sell you something. They are genuinely interested in helping you, not just getting you to use the Google product line.

Here is a short list of groups related to Google where you can find help and support:

Adwords Help - http://groups.google.com/group/adwords-help

Gmail Help - http://groups.google.com/group/Gmail-Help-Discussion

Google Base Help - http://groups.google.com/group/base-help-discussion

Blogger Help - http://groups.google.com/group/blogger-help

Adsense Help - http://groups.google.com/group/adsense-help

Google Groups Guide - http://groups.google.com/group/Google-Groups-Guide

Google Page Creator - http://groups.google.com/
group/GPCDiscussionGroup

Let me stress here that these groups can really help you.
You won't see the hyped up crap you sometimes see on the
internet. You'll find real information here. Use it to your
advantage. It will make you money. Play by Google's rules, and
Google will give you the love! Google wants you to succeed.
You make money using their services, and they make money.
It's really win-win.

If you don't already have a Gmail account, you'll need to
sign up for one. Once you have a Gmail account, you'll need to
log in because you can't get the information you need about
groups unless you're already signed in.

Your next step is to search groups to look for groups that
are relevant to your topic. You can also browse through the
group categories to find groups you are looking for.

Some groups will only allow you to see the archives if
you join, so you may have to subscribe and unsubscribe from
some groups in order to tell if the group is right for you.

Now, here is an example search:

I chose the term "submit articles" because I am looking
for groups to submit my articles to.

Here is a short list of sites I found:

article_announce

Submit and Reprint **Articles** for your website, ezines, and any online publications for free!

Join now to reprint and **submit**!
Category: Arts and Entertainment > Literature, Language: English
High activity, 80 members, restricted

articlesender
This group is intended to help publishers get quality **articles** to reprint for their site, books, and etc.

Writers **submit** your **articles**, free of charge.

REMINDER: Publishers be sure to include the author's byline/resource box/about the author bio with all URLs hyperlinked/active.
Category: Business and Finance > Small Business, Language: English
High activity, 195 members, moderated, restricted

articlebank
This group is intended to help publishers get quality **articles** to reprint for their site, books, and etc.

Writers **submit** your **articles**, free of charge.

REMINDER: Publishers be sure to include the author's byline/resource box/about the author bio with all URLs hyperlinked/active.
Category: Other, Language: English
High activity, 49 members, moderated, restricted

freecontentarticles
This group is intended to help publishers get quality **articles** to reprint for their site, books, and etc.

Writers **submit** your **articles**, free of charge.

REMINDER: Publishers be sure to include the author's byline/resource box/about the author bio with all URLs hyperlinked/active.

Category: <u>Computers</u> > <u>Databases</u>, Language: <u>English</u>
High activity, 46 members, moderated, restricted

free-reprintable-**articles**

This group is intended to help publishers get quality **articles** to reprint for their site, books, and etc.

Writers **submit** your **articles**, free of charge.

REMINDER: Publishers be sure to include the author's byline/resource box/about the author bio with all URLs hyperlinked/active.

Category: <u>Other</u>, Language: <u>English</u>
High activity, 124 members, moderated, restricted

Free Content

Get free content for your website, newsletters or print. Authors can **submit** their free **articles**. Web editors seeking **articles** can post their needs for **articles** here. Contributing writers: Please provide contact information and any usage information with your **articles**.

Category: <u>Computers</u> > <u>Internet</u>
Low activity, 301 members

free-**article**-content

This group is for writers who want to **submit** their **articles** for webmasters to publish, and for webmasters who are looking for free **articles** which they can reprint in their ezines and/or websites.

Language: <u>English</u>
High activity, 382 members

Weight Loss for women

Any topic on weight loss and loosing weight,join ,ask and support other weight loss members.this group is opean to everyone
and you can **submit** or post any **article** dealing with weight loss

Low activity, 125 members

Submit Your **Articles** Here

We accept free reprint **articles** and content on all topics. We do not permit pure advertising.

Please review thePhantomWriters **Article** Submission & Usage Guidelines:
(http://thephantomwriters.com/x.pl/tpw/info/groups/index.html)
These rules will be enforced.
Category: Arts and Entertainment, Language: English
Low activity, 200 members, moderated

.NET Studio

This is a developer group which helps developers to search for source codes on .net platform and find out better solutions for their projects. It is open for ideas and good logix. One can ask questions; **submit** suggestions, **articles**, source codes, architectures and other helpful materials.
Category: Computers > Operating Systems, Language: English
Low activity, 87 members

Publish These **Articles**

This group is intended to help publishers get quality **articles** to reprint for their site, books, and etc.

Writers **submit** your **articles**, free of charge.

REMINDER: Publishers be sure to include the author's byline/resource box/about the author bio with all URLs hyperlinked/active.
Category: Arts and Entertainment > Literature, Language: English
High activity, 109 members

Article Submission

Free **Articles Submit**/View. Free **Article** Submission sites brought to you by one of the leading free **article** site. http://www.fortuneinfo.com/ArticleSite. All new members signing up at http://www.fortuneinfo.com/ArticleSite/ will receive a free e-book on Affiliate Marketing.
Language: English
Low activity, 3 members

Account Managers

Account Managers get account management best-practices at Account Managers MarketPlace. **Submit** your press releases and **articles** for free marketing. Learn account management standards.

Category: Business and Finance > Marketplace, Language: English
Low activity, 6 members

home-audio-video-**articles**
Home Audio & Video. We will accept reviews, how-to manuals & technical papers. Only **submit** free reprint Audio Video **articles**

Please review thePhantomWriters **Article** Submission & Usage Guidelines:
(http://thephantomwriters.com/x.pl/tpw/info/groups/index.html)
These rules will be enforced..
Category: Arts and Entertainment > Television, Language: English
Low activity, 16 members

(This is only an example search. Groups change from time to time, so conduct your own searches regularly so you can add and delete groups from your list of groups.)

This list gives me the number of members, the activity of the groups, as well as the group category so that I can use this information to search for other related groups on this topic.

You'll also find out what language the group is in. This is important so that you can either find groups in other languages besides English, or you can find English only groups.

Here is another search I did for groups that offer free classified ads:

alt.**ads**.forsale - Show matching messages from this group

Category: Other, Language: English

Low activity, 52 subscribers, Usenet

Ottawa classifieds (for anyone in the Ottawa surrounding area)
This newsgroup is **free** and is intended for anyone in the
Ottawa and surrounding areas to place **free classified ads**.

 Thank You

Language: English
Low activity, 25 members

Free Classified Ads Classifieds
The most comprehensive **free classified ads** on the web.
Place unlimited number of **classified ads** for **free** in just a few
seconds. No registration required.
Visit **Classified Ads** 4 **Free**!
Language: English
Low activity, 83 members

Park_Drive
100s of hot-selling product ideas, How to rank #1 in the search
engines, **Free** and low-cost online **classified ads** that produce
sales, Making sales instantly with online auctions like eBay,
Getting links from 100s of high-traffic sites, How to spend less
than 20 minutes per day running your business!
Category: Business and Finance, Language: English (UK)
Low activity, 13 members

cheeringup **classified ads**
Post an **ad** or search for something to make your life easier and
better. **Free** advertising for members. Your **classified ad**
can be posted easily. Join this group FOR IMMEDIATE **FREE**
ADVERTISING.

Category: Other, Language: English
Low activity, 55 members, restricted

iQuest **Classified Ads**
Welcome to iQuest **Classified Ads** Online

All individual entrepreneurs are welcome, post anything you want for **free** like affiliate adverstising, small business, mlm and etc., excluding pornography.

Category: Other, Language: English
Low activity, 4 members

Ads Solution California
http://go2-url.com/aaauaz/
http://go2-url.com/aaauad/
http://go2-url.com/aaaurs/
Get your **Free Classified ADs** on 12 Million+ Sites and in 72 Million+ Spam **Free** Emails. Also get a **Free** FFA Links Page with **Free** Submitter. This Submitter submits your link to the entire FreeAds2000 network with one
Category: Asia > China, Language: English
Low activity, 1 member

Ads Solution Denmark
http://go2-url.com/aaauaz/
http://go2-url.com/aaauad/
http://go2-url.com/aaaurs/
Get your **Free Classified ADs** on 12 Million+ Sites and in 72 Million+ Spam **Free** Emails. Also get a **Free** FFA Links Page with **Free** Submitter. This Submitter submits your link to the entire FreeAds2000 network with one
Category: Asia > Bahrain, Language: English
Low activity, 1 member

CLASSIFIED EXTRA MARITAL AFFAIRS
Secret Affairs. Looking for sexxy women to have extra marital affairs with. No Strings Attached. Serving San Francisco Bay Area. Minumum qualifications are over age of 18, you must look good in jeans and disease **free** and you have to be ready to have a blast. Thanks for looking.
Category: Adult > Sex, Language: English
Low activity, 17 members

Free Adult Sex **Ads** Thailand
http://mimi1a.resourcez.com
http://resourcez.com/mimi1a

Get your **Free Classified ADs** on 12 Million+ Sites and in 72 Million+ Spam **Free** Emails. Also get a **Free** FFA Links Page with **Free** Submitter. This Submitter submits your link to the entire FreeAds2000 network with one click!100% **FREE**!

Category: Adult > Businesses, Language: Thai

Low activity, 4 members

Free Sex **Classified Ads** Thailand

http://mimi1a.resourcez.com

http://resourcez.com/mimi1a

Get your **Free Classified ADs** on 12 Million+ Sites and in 72 Million+ Spam **Free** Emails. Also get a **Free** FFA Links Page with **Free** Submitter. This Submitter submits your link to the entire FreeAds2000 network with one click!100% **FREE**!

Category: Business and Finance > Business Services, Language: Thai

Low activity, 1 member

Free Ads Solution Thailand

http://mimi1a.radpages.com

http://radpages.com/mimi1a

Get your **Free Classified ADs** on 12 Million+ Sites and in 72 Million+ Spam **Free** Emails. Also get a **Free** FFA Links Page with **Free** Submitter. This Submitter submits your link to the entire FreeAds2000 network with one click!100% **FREE**!

Category: Other, Language: Thai

Low activity, 1 member

VisitOurWebSites

Tell everyone about your web site. It's **free** advertising for all members. Post **ad** tips and ideas. No imoral junk or anti religious stuff. Only info suitable for families. After you join, place **free classified** adds on the web to invite others. Put a link to this group in your website.

Category: Business and Finance > Entrepeneurs, Language: English

Low activity, 20 members, moderated

Cognigen Networking

Agents needed

* Affiliations
* Autoresponders
* Banner Exchanges
* **Classified Ads**
* E-commerce
* E-zines
* **Free** For All Link Pages
* Link Exchanges

http://wilcoxson.cognigen.org/
Low activity, 3 members

West Michigan Deals
West Michigan Deals and Classifieds. All of the best local deals on merchandise, gas, food and services. There is also a **classified ads** section to place **FREE ads**.
Language: English
Low activity, 4 members

Now, what this tells me is that I will probably have to tweak my search criteria a little more so that I can find places that accept ads on my particular products and services.

When you're submitting to groups, you want to make sure the message you are submitting is appropriate to the group you are submitting to. Don't get yourself banned because you submitted to the wrong group.

Also, you want to make sure that you add a signature to your posts. Most groups will accept a signature file, which is similar to a resource box in your articles, and this is where you will advertise your products and services. Just make sure you write a good signature file, and keep it brief.

How often you submit is also key here. With article, ad, or any type of promotional group, you may be limited on how often you can submit. Some will allow you to submit daily; others weekly, or on some other type of schedule. Follow the rules to get better results.

Once you understand the terms of use of each group you are posting to, you can speed up your posting by using tools like **Group Mail**, http://www.infacta.com/. (They do offer a free version, and this should be sufficient for your group marketing campaigns.)

The way to do this is to create groups within Group Mail specifically related to the types of promotions you are doing.

For example, if you are posting articles, you can create an article group. Add all of the email addresses for the different groups you are a member of, then copy and paste your message and send.

When setting up Group Mail, it's important to make sure that you set your settings to SMTP. You don't want to use Bulk Mail mode because Google will see your messages as spam. By using the SMTP mode, you are sending the messages individually. Although this does take a little longer, it's worth it because your messages will get accepted.

Using software to send your messages will take a lot of tedium out of marketing on groups. Because it saves you time, you can market more in less time. This will help you increase your sales.

Blogger – http://www.blogger.com/

If you want to create a blog for your business, and you don't want the hassles of building a website, you can always create a blog. What makes a blog so great is that it's easy to organize your information, and it's very easy to build. All you have to do is decide what you want the topic of your blog to be, set it up, and then you can start posting to your blog in minutes.

Another advantage to creating a blog is if you only market affiliate programs and don't want to build a website. Sites like Ezine Articles and Search Warp only allow you to include links to your own websites now. The way to work around this is to create a blog.

To get the most out of your blog, try to post at least three times a week, and allow your subscribers to subscribe through both email and RSS. This can help you dramatically increase the number of readers you have.

With Blogger, it makes it easy for you to get indexed by Google. Google owns Blogger, so they spider this site regularly. This is especially important if you are having trouble getting your sites into Google and building backlinks.

Here are several tips for building your blog using Blogger:

1. Stick with a simple theme. A cute theme is fine if you're building a personal blog, or you're not running a site related to business. If you're running a business site though, you want to stick with something that's simple, clean, and looks professional.

2. Write a complete profile. The problem with the internet is that it can be very impersonal. Credibility is everything if you want to make the sale. If you have one, include your picture on your site. This can actually help increase readership and sales.

3. Include as many feed options as possible for your readers. Some will want to subscribe through RSS. Others will want to subscribe through email. You can use a system like **Feedblitz**, **http://www.feedlblitz.com/**, to offer an email subscription to your blog. If you want to add as many options as possible for subscribing through RSS, then use **Feedburner**, **http://www.feedburner.com/**. Not only does this site allow you to create buttons you can quickly copy and paste onto your blog, but it also

allows you to optimize your feed for syndication on other sites, and your feed can be read as a web page. Feedburner also offers an email option too.

4. You will need to ping your blog manually. I would suggest you use one of the ping services to do this.

5. Post regularly to your blog. Once you build your readership, you want to give them information to read so they don't forget about you. The downside of the internet is that you need to constantly remind others you exist.

Part 2
Hot Marketing Technique:
Social Bookmarking

One of the most important techniques you can apply to your business is linking. This is an excellent technique for raising your rankings in the search engines and building traffic, especially if you hate to write. All you have to do is write a description of the appropriate page and submit your link for inclusion in directories.

The problem with linking though is that it's very time consuming. As a one person business owner, I can tell you that it's a good idea to automate as much as you possibly can. You also want to use as many time saving tools as you can. Below are my best tips on linking using the latest in linking.

Now, what's hot in linking these days is social bookmarking sites. Social bookmarking sites are basically sites that allow you to create lists of sites you've visited. In other words, bookmarks. In fact, it's a simple and easy way to organize your bookmarks.

There are several problems here though. If you have as many sites as I do, and you have as many pages of content as I do, then it can take awhile to get all of your pages bookmarked. Also, I believe you will get better results from having others recommend your site.

Your first step to getting started with this is to sign up for an account with **Only Wire**, http://www.onlywire.com/.

The reason you want an account with this site is so that you can get your site on several bookmarking sites all at once, and you can do some of your own bookmarking so your site is linked to this site.

This will speed up your submissions and get you included much more quickly than if you work with one account at a time. Even if you write your description first, you will still have to copy and paste it at least 15 times. You want to post to several networks all at once.

Once you've set up your Only Wire account, your next step is to sign up for individual accounts. Add your usernames and passwords to Only Wire. Then, add a button to your browser. Once you've done this, then you can start bookmarking your websites.

One thing Only Wire doesn't include is **Digg**, http://www.digg.com/ so you'll want to get an account here.

Digg is the highest ranking social bookmarking site on the internet. In fact, it ranks in the top 100 sites online. It gets a lot of traffic, so you will want to sign up for an account on this site too. You will need to put your description in a text document so you can copy and paste it to this bookmark site. You can get a **Digg account** for free: http://www.digg.com/. Once you've finished bookmarking your main sites with Only Wire, then bookmark them with Digg so you can get included there.

Now, you will want to add a button to your website or blog so others can bookmark your site. The easiest way to do this is to use **Add This**, http://www.addthis.com/. This site makes most of the bookmarking sites available, including Digg,

Setting up an Add This account is pretty straightforward. You don't even need an account unless you want statistics.

Your first step is to go to the middle of the page and click on: Get the Web Buttons. Next, choose the type of widget. If it's for your website, then you should choose Bookmarking Widget. If you want a button for your feed, then choose feed. Choose the type of button you want. Then choose whether you want it on your website or your blog.

If you want statistics, you'll need an account, but it's very fast and easy to sign up for. Then, click Get Your Free Button.

Copy and paste this code on your site. I would recommend that you put it somewhere close to your menu and in a very prominent place so that visitors to your site see it.

Bonus Tools and Resources

These are the latest tools and resources I've found to help you with marketing your site. Their purpose is to help you increase your marketing efforts, save you time, and also save you money on tools you may need. Best of all, all of these tools are free, and they will make your job a whole lot easier.

Google and Google Adwords

Adwords Editor -
http://www.google.com/intl/en/adwordseditor/index.html

Making the Most Out of Your Google Adwords Account -
http://www.google.com/ads/library/maximimum_effect_dec03.pdf – Written by the Google Adwords team. This short report contains worksheets to help you determine your goals with Adwords as well as worksheets for helping you write your ads.

Google Adwords and Yahoo PPC Tips -
http://www.seobook.com/overture-adwords.pdf – More tips for writing pay per click ads.

Google Adwords Made Easy –
http://www.askjinger.com/keywordsearch/adwordsma

deeasy.zip – Written by expert internet marketer Brad Callen, this ebook is the best ebook I've seen on writing ads for Google Adwords.

Google Documents - http://docs.google.com/ - Use this site to upload, share, and edit your word processing and spreadsheet documents.

Sitemaps Pal - http://www.sitemapspal.com/ - Use this tool to create a sitemap for both Google and Yahoo.

Google Pack - http://pack.google.com/ - Free software you can download and use on your computer.

Search Engine Optimization

SEO Made Easy -

http://www.askjinger.com/seo/seomadeeasy.zip –

Brad Callen's SEO course on search engine optimization. This course has some of the best information I've seen on optimizing your site for the search engines, and he shows you how to choose keywords using the software Good Keywords, which is free: http://www.goodkeywords.com.

What you learn here you can also use when writing articles, ads, or anything else that needs to be optimized for the search engines because this information will help you choose the correct keywords.

More Marketing Tools

VRE Toolbar - http://www.vretoolbar.com/ - Indispensable tool for any business owner, especially affiliates, to do research for your business.

Ultimate Internet Marketing Toolbar - http://www.xeal.com/tools/toolbar/getbar.htm - This toolbar contains hundreds of tools you can use, and it includes submission tools to help you submit your site.

Only Wire - http://www.onlywire.com/ - Free online tool you can use to bookmark your websites and blogs to 15 different social bookmarking sites.

Socializer - http://www.socializer.com/ - Semi-automated bookmarking to 44 different social bookmarking sites.

Social Bookmarks Manager - http://www.socialbookmarksmanager.com/ - Lets you create bookmarks code for all of your pages, not just blogs.

31 Bookmarking Sites - http://bloggerwhale.blogspot.com/2007/02/ive-been-blogging-around-for-sometime.html - Includes the Alexa rankings for these sites.

Robin Good's Social Bookmarking List -
http://www.masternewmedia.org/news/2006/12/01/s
ocial_bookmarking_services_and_tools.htm

Article Manager -
http://www.freedownloadmanager.org/downloads/Arti
cle_Manager_46969_p/ - Use this free tool to organize your
articles, as well as submit to the major directories.

Free Article Software -
http://www.freearticlesoftware.com/ - helps you organize
your articles, as well as submit custom, original articles to the
top 100 article directories.

Article Marketer –
http://www.askjinger.com/am/

- This is the service I use to submit all of my articles because
it's computer independent, meaning it's an online service you
can reach through your browser. They offer a free version
where you can submit up to 3 articles per week. Each article will
be submitted to 29 directories and over 11,000 publishers.
You'll also get the 8 minute article writing software to help you
write your articles, as well as Article Marketer University to
teach you how to get the most from your article writing efforts.
Both of these resources are free.

www.ingramcontent.com/pod-product-compliance
Lightning Source LLC
Chambersburg PA
CBHW051249170526
45165CB00004B/1639